Killing María

A Poem for Multiple Voices

Queridos Luis y Trimi,

Claudia Castro Luna

Con esperanza y Justicia

[signature]

Two Sylvias Press

Two Sylvias Press
PO Box 1524
Kingston, WA 98346
twosylviaspress@gmail.com

Cover Artist: Charles Spitzack
Cover Design: Kelli Russell Agodon
Book Design: Annette Spaulding-Convy
Author Photo Credit: Timothy Aguero

Artist Charles Spitzack is dedicated to dissolving barriers in commitment to the communal whole. Based out of Seattle for the past 10 years, he is a graduate of Cornish College of the Arts and has an AAS degree from Seattle Central College's Wood Technology Center. He is represented by Davidson Galleries. http://www.cspitzack.com

Created with the belief that great writing is good for the world, Two Sylvias Press mixes modern technology, classic style, and literary intellect with an eco-friendly heart. We draw our inspiration from the poetic literary talent of Sylvia Plath and the editorial business sense of Sylvia Beach. We are an independent press dedicated to publishing the exceptional voices of writers.

First Edition. Created in the United States of America.

ISBN: 978-0-9986314-4-8

Two Sylvias Press
www.twosylviaspress.com

Praise for *Killing Marías*

Each poem in *Killing Marías* is addressed to someone named María who has been killed in Juárez. Lyric in tradition, they are more love poems than elegies. The poems are full of love, of care, of transnational empathy. This is a book that is unusually moving and beautifully written.

> — Juliana Sphar, author of nine books of poetry, including *This Connection of Everyone with Lungs, Well Then There Now,* and *That Winter the Wolf Came*

જી

In this epic poetry collection *Killing Marías*, Claudia Castro Luna, both poetically and physically, settles spaces that were unclaimed by Latinas. Her inscription of the disappeared women of Juárez is a live cartographic image of struggle and spiritual survival. Castro Luna does not allow for these dead women to lack agency; they nourish us and the earth, and they speak with their bodies, literally, positioning themselves as recovered entities with agency, in the poet's skilled narrativizing hands.

> — Gabriella Gutiérrez y Muhs, Ph.D., author of *A Most Improbable Life* and *The Runaway Poems: A Manual of Love*

જી

In *Killing Marías*, each poem is a rosary bead named after a woman's life in Ciudad Juárez. Each bead reveals a crack of light through which we can peak into the hurt so many women experience from birth to death. Castro Luna's piercing voice states "exploitation has no limits," and that "man's hypocrisy even less." She dares us to stop being mediocre humans, especially men, and let the "feminine thrive."

> — Javier Zamora, author of *Unaccompanied* and *Nueve Años Inmigrantes / Nine Immigrant Years*

Acknowledgments

Above all I want to acknowledge the women and girls who have been murdered in Juárez, Mexico and the friends and families who loved them and miss them everyday.

Gracias de puro corazón, to Gabriella Gutiérrez y Muhs for her heartfelt and insightful foreword and to Charles Spitzack for his generosity of spirit and time etching the beautiful cover.

Thank you to the women and men in Elmaz Abinader's 2013 VONA workshop for their thoughtful feedback, to MALCS (Mujeres Activas en Letras y Cambio Social) for their support during the 2015 Albuquerque Summer Institute and to La Sala, a Puget Sound Latinx arts collective, for giving me the opportunity to perform the poem in its entirety during their 2016 La Cocina project.

Extiendo gracias a mi compatriota y amigo Javier Zamora—que la belleza te acompañe siempre.

With appreciation to Juliana Spahr for her words and brilliant teaching.

Mil gracias para Wendy Call for her wisdom and editing support.

My most heartfelt thanks to Kelli Russell Agodon and Annette Spaulding-Convy for believing in this work.

Finally, endless gratitude to my husband Sean Heron and my children Amalia, Sofía, and Lucas for walking with me along this creative journey.

From the onset of my writing these poems I have felt my hand guided at times by the dead women whose names appear in the text. These are their poems as much as they are mine. In that spirit, I will donate the royalties I earn to organizations defending Women's Rights on the US-Mexico border.

Table of Contents

Foreword

Reclaiming Marías: Claudia The Medium

In this epic poetry collection *Killing Marías*, Claudia Castro Luna, both poetically and physically, settles spaces previously unclaimed by Latinas. Her inscription of the disappeared women of Juárez is a live cartographic image of struggle and spiritual survival vis à vis the erased history of femicide/femicidio. The wound the border represents is in Castro Luna's hands not only an open wound as Chicana author and theorist Gloria Anzaldúa named the borderlands, but a scar with the names of Marías as intricate, meaningful and compelling stitches, or is it letters? earth tattoos? that culturally scaffold a justice skeleton for the killed, tortured, brutalized and largely invisibilized women of the border.

In no other part of the world would the lives of more than six hundred young and healthy women become an unnamed historical period. It is important to clarify that numbers are blurred, that we have not even bothered to count the numbers of women killed. Claudia Castro Luna does not allow for these dead women to lack agency; they nourish us and the earth, and they speak with their bodies, literally, positioning themselves as recovered entities with agency, in the poet's skilled hands.

Poets are expected to be the canaries in the coalmine, to test the waters, to act as empaths of current and relatable feelings, or experiences, the population possesses and to identify what the world does not. They are visionaries, they are to report on all the perceptions that no one else can see, and are charged with being able to visualize a better future by improving the world, and if nothing else, by reporting.

Claudia Castro Luna does not disappoint us in *Killing Marías*, but instead, as the medium between us worldly creatures, and the victims of monumental and yet minimized criminality, she transforms. Castro Luna, the poet, gives us the opportunity to listen, when we didn't in the past, to absolve ourselves from our positions of participants instead of mere collaborators of an abuse, by simply not howling about this genocide in Juárez that began in the early 1990s.

An entire world witnessed the development of two cartels, the Juárez and Sinaloa, literally ripping holes through the state of Chihuahua, where Juárez is located, in order to cut it in half. According to *National Geographic*, from 2008-2012 Ciudad Juárez was "widely deemed to be the most dangerous place on Earth." In 2010 alone, almost four thousand people were killed. The quantities of dead people vary, and few articles focus especially on the fact that this is a femicide, a killing of mostly women, thus Claudia Castro Luna's title to this poetry collection: *Killing Marías*.

The significance of the title is tremendous because what Mexicans have called "Marías" have been almost exclusively indigenous women, who have labored in middle class homes, mostly for mestizos and/or people who consider themselves of a higher class. To most Mexicans "Marías," are synonyms for an indigenous domestic worker. The name is loaded. It is both the mother of Jesus and the name of mothers of many bastard children, the fruit of silenced rapes. A society has allowed for these women to be abused, both physically and sexually by turning a blind eye, for more than five hundred years. These are the poor, indigenous women who in Mexico have been historically condescended and invisibilized. It is thus essential that their cries become a chant "in multiple voices" as the poet indicates.

As Gloria Anzaldúa noted, the border is a wound that cannot heal. Ciudad Juárez is a terrain I know well; the only picture of me as a baby was taken at the Chamizal Park, by a fotógrafo ambulante (street photographer). In "María de Jesús Mother of Weeping Rocks," Castro Luna, claims the Chamizal, a historically disputed land in Juárez that had been polemically taken away from Mexico for one hundred years and then given back to Mexico in 1964. One of the María protagonists is found dead in this land. The poet subverts this crime and reformulates the tortured mother's body, which provides mother's milk, as a healer of the land, while making this maternal body into a "holy night." By paralleling the body of a woman, not valued by a culture that treasures the other María, the Virgin, and protagonist of the "holy night," the Mother of God, Castro Luna poetically and elegantly elevates the bodies of the hundreds of victims of Juárez, into a status of survivors with agency, power and possibility.

The importance of these poems is three-pronged, for the dead, disappeared and invisibilized: not only is Castro Luna raising the dead women killed and disappeared in/on the border, the ones found, and the ones still missing, but she is also focusing attention on a land of crossings where varied cultures have cohabited, and where many border crossers-including a great number of women have lost their lives, (crossing into the "United States").

This is another reason for which we are also part of this manuscript: as Americans who have benefited from the services of women who work for less than minimum wage to provide their labor, risking their lives in so doing, criminalized by a country that benefits from them. We co-exist, the subaltern country, producer of Marías, and the "patron/master" country that refuses to take responsibility for utilizing these subaltern beings, products of both countries, in order to improve its livability:

"María Santos Sweetest Apple"

They say we live
on either side of a border

I say that's fodder
for a sexist imagination

coyote's tooth does not alone bite
and falcon's feather takes not alone to the sky

silo living is not for living things

like the braid on my abuela's back
and beads on a Rosary strand

interlinked we are rain, dust, stars

We have benefited from lower costs for daycare, hotels, fast food, and elder care, because the Marías that cross the border are able to provide this cheap labor. I give this analysis because I am the niece and daughter of six women named María as their first given name and possessing an additional second name, as is the case in rural Mexico. The second or middle name is the one that counts oftentimes for the families. But, the metaphor is also here, part of this story; we have not yet figured out as a nation that "María" is the preamble to another name.

The women given voice in Castro Luna's poems have spilled over to heal us. They bring balms, knowledge, wisdom, a legacy of hard work, spirituality and we are able in the poet's hands to

Hear in the void

the echo of her

(From "María Teresa Greatest Ancestor")

—Gabriella Gutiérrez y Muhs, Ph.D., author of *A Most Improbable Life* and *The Runaway Poems: A Manual of Love*

Written in memory of women and girls
killed in Ciudad Juárez, Mexico
and
for all women and girls who are
victims of domestic violence

María

Somos todas una
protégenos madrecita

We are all one
in your image made
hermanas
linked, backstitched
to the edge of your brilliant robe

Like you
we have aureolas
smooth and nipples hard
like you
we have a nested swallow cave
and a life-giving cut

All about you
is harmonious and divine
nacre of the deepest ocean
star of purple skies
your divinity surges
inside each of us

María Agustina Mystical Rose

Dearly Beloveds,
women's names
pebbles under a stream
flowing out to sea
hold them in your mouth
taste the oval shapes
their perfect randomness
taste the bitter and salt
petal and sweet
ears cannot touch
what tongues can see

María Ascensión Crater of Solitude

María, you are now dead
nothing of you left
meet me
in this place at the back of my hand
where footprints leave no marks
meet me
in the sinuous valleys
between these printed ridges
safe, the coolness of the page
my words are shelter
and leave no room
for men's fears nor blame

María Cristina Hanging Chrysalis

What would I do
for a smidgeon
of your rebellion, María?
As a woman to trust
the halo of your intuition
I know you know
courage plummets
easily from cliffs of doubt
both imposed and self harvested—
how to make manifest
what the mind knows
but the eye cannot yet see?
How to pluck Hope
from the terraced gardens
where it grows?
I think about the nature of change
the transfiguration of grain to woman
the audacity of salt to embolden water into ocean
the urge to break free

María de Jesús Mother of Rain

There in the mirror
staring me down
is you
from the place
where love burns
and roads meet

María de Jesús Mother of Weeping Rocks

It starts early
before you learn to speak
even before
you leave the hospital
in your mother's arms
that your body is not your own
that women's paychecks are cut short
that women's wombs remain law controlled
you'd think after all these years
things would be different
the pink that casts your gender
a diaphanous cage
passing as rosy charm
a fine chainmail
to be worn at all times

María de la Luz Gracious Serpent

The light left your eyes, Luz,
you, who were enshrined in it at birth
for some women
light—lux, is a luxury
spilled from untold pores

María de los Ángeles Heaven's Nest

Exploitation has no limits
man's hypocrisy even less

human history is smeared
with the filth of their spread

nefarious tentacles grip
everything from politics to jeans

all that denim walking New York and LA streets
cut and sewn in places like Ciudad Juárez and Bangladesh

do you, Beloved, know
whose fingerprints trace the clothes you wear?

inside maquilas, grim labor camps,
hands flutter at racing speed

women darning garments, stitching bras, shirts, jeans
propelling fashion industry's fickle needs

fingers swollen with aching, mother's fingers, daughter's fingers
bent, warped fingers, appendages to sugarless hands

María de los Ángeles Boundless Love

Always question
what remains
blame not fallen angels
the answer is here on earth
emblazoned
on duplicitous tongues
let it be said,
the snake bites its tail
and love and hate
connect

María de los Ángeles Fiercest Fire

Ay, Sister,
Jasmine blooms
in my garden
the fragrance rides
comets' backs
it reaches stars
and the hearts
of sons and daughters
you left at 65

María de Lourdes Song of Plenty

When the belt
seared me that time
the sun inside me burst
corn yellow
urine streamed down
scorching my raw legs
swollen in ridges
from his lashings

I was four, maybe five
when darkness settled
wounded and shameful
in a corner of the universe
held by my ribcage
but my tongue, winged bug,
saved itself and flew
to perch atop the moon

I thirst. Yet, for all the light I drink
the now grey/black
discoloration around my ribs
cannot brighten.
Still, my tongue has grown
is now a winged and taloned beast
and on clear nights
it comes home to roost

María del Refugio Virgen Most Powerful

153 eggs at birth
sublime secrets
inside a baby girl's innermost whorl
each ready to fulfill life's mystery
María del Refugio
your promise only three years old
a dried bud now—due to a killer's ploy

María Maynez Hermana de la Montaña

Hold with me
a minute of silence

(Uno)

(Dos)

(Tres)

(Cuatro)

(Cinco)

(Seis)

(Siete)

(Ocho)

(Nueve)

(Diez)

Hear in the void
The   echo   of   her

María del Rosario Merciful Virgin

Love me
Love me not
Love me
Love me not
Ah margarita,
Dear daisy,
what is it
that people
we love,
and need,
so often
destroy us?

María Most Wise

Violence tears
and its tears
soak pillows
puddle church altars
dam bus stops
dampen evening suppers
flood cul-de-sacs
mourning waters swell
to wailing rivers
beneath city streets

María E. Dweller of Heaven

After 43 years, lead took you María, to eternal oblivion
The guilty ones run free, protected by official oblivion

María E. Queen of Lullabies

Bajo tus pies pétalos de rosa,
en tus tiernos oídos canciones de corazón
en cada dedo anillos dorados
y en tu bolsillo todo mi amor

María Elba Queen of Angels

Did someone ever
tell you,
that the winning
lottery ticket
was you?

María Elena Mirror of Justice

You at 15
your head smashed
your nails blood blue
o dead virgin
was it a nightingale
a bald eagle
or a ruiseñor?
On whose feathers
did you travel
to the sky above?

María Elena Throne of Wisdom

The one who shot you María
is not son of a bitch
whores birth tenderness
like the rest of us
with a slit between our legs

.

María Estela Cause of our Joy

Investors insist
on profits high
shoppers insist
on prices low
greed and ignorance
breed ordered pairs
cold economics
on a Cartesian plane
but working women
are thinking women
are feeling women
with mouths to feed
with dreams to seek
and life to love

María Estela Spirit Shrine

Your field of light waned
Queen Firefly

I hold you in mine
porque somos la misma

María Eugenia Harvest Tower

María, your rose
on a shallow grave

the desert refused
to swallow your dew

María Inéz House of Gold

María, stardust
blessed your face

as it darkened
into eternal night

María Irma Gate of Heaven

Anguish rushing downriver
chafing boulder and rock
grinding agony to foam
drowned your scream
without a chance
to reach anyone who cared
while some of us
reached by catalogs bloated
with offers to buy stuff
reached by television
airing nothing more than fluff

María Irma Morning Star

If you a knife
could wield
would you
slice the balls
of he who killed you
and eat them
con chile y limón,
hair and all?

María Isabel Health of the Sick

Maggots feast
on carrion
eventually
develop wings
bones carry on

María Isabel Hug of the Earth

Pensive they sit on telephone wires like apparitions from the beyond. Winged creatures, evolutionary mutants, birds habit in two worlds. They sing with breath of the living and stain wing tips with death's dust. When bodies get buried, souls climb to the heavens. Birds greet these newly dead on their way up where there are no harsh edges, no adrenaline, only time. Bird, bird is. Blissful and plaintive, birds sing on earth, sing in heaven, the same songs.

María Isabel Boulder of Strength

There is no limit
some kill
some bank
some drink
some buy
some watch
some stand by
the playing hand
the poaching game
that killed her
Beloveds!
see wholly her figure
behind the hours
Justice awaits

María Isabel Cup of Morning Sun

How many among us
bear marks
blue green, blue green
like gasoline rainbows
under long-sleeve shirts?

How many among us
bear marks
abuse watermarks
in the lining
of a lukewarm smile?

How many among us
swing between
courage
and defeat
in the span
of a day?
In the span
of an hour?
In the swing
of a second?

María Isela Balm of Tenderness

The onslaught
at the supermarket checkout line
lips, breasts, legs, skin
dismembered women
selling inane products
planting distrust
María, balm of tenderness,
heal our bodies
mend clefts of self-doubt
make resolute our hearts
guard the seed
from whence all things start

María Warrior of Self

Sometimes
when I wake up
soft and more
of dream
than waking life
I wish
to lick myself
the way a cat
cleanses—
my tongue
over the miracle
of my hands
over the soft plane
that is my belly
down the length
of my legs
my tongue lapping
tender over
my calloused feet
—especially over
my calloused feet
licking with devotion
the arable land
of my back
scooping
the forgotten sweat
behind my knees
seeing what is there to see
the edges at the mouth
the cave that brought
my children forth into life
my tongue over my territory
the way a cat knows
the limits of her fur

María Luisa Ark of the Covenant

Guns and knives
slice names
scorch dreams
excoriate faith
make
Spring resurrections
Summer plenties
Fall harvests
Winter devotions
mean nothing
aslant roads
sullied memories
and yet
feet on uneven ground
women meet
themselves
each day

María Luisa y sus Tres Niños Fiercest of Mothers

They left you, María Luisa, with your three children
to be found by dogs
your dried womb
their hungry bellies
no more

María Maura Healer of Headaches

A small bird,
I don't know what kind,
has made its nest
underneath the swell
of my unmowed grass
three tiny eggs
inside an impeccably
woven basket
she trusted the spot—
In kind, the children
have left her alone
that is all
a safe patch
to be left alone
to nourish ourselves
and raise our young

María Rocío Cosmic Vision

Beloveds,
consider
the privilege
of reading
these lines

María Rosa Sister of Spring

I write of you
my wrist against
misogynist fists
punching day and night

I write of you
the echo of your scream
harnessed
by my yellow pencil

I place you
in this rose garden
nothing really blue
just notes
soaked with life

María Rosario Clearest of Nights

How to makeup with yourself
after each self breakup?
How to cuddle under a broken wing
the girl of you?
Or how to explain
that deep inside the sea
sister wind tries on her dress?
Snails leave their homes
when no one is looking
and birds sometimes are afraid to fly
who is going to tell you
what you only know?
Whose fool will tell spider
to spin less?
It turns out that it is possible
to mend the crevices inside yourself
without silk threads and silver spoons
it is possible to tell the truth
and not burn in hell
to win wars without shooting a rifle
and without a rifle to write a poem

María Sagrario Food to the Hungry

One of you
was already
too many

who cares
if desert sand
wells heat
into night

for a corpse
warmth
dusk, dawn
moon, sun

is naught

María Santos Sweetest Apple

They say we live
on either side of a border

I say that's fodder
for a sexist imagination

coyote's tooth does not alone bite
and falcon's feather takes not alone to the sky

silo living is not for living things

like the braid on my abuela's back
and beads on a Rosary strand

interlinked we are rain, dust, stars

María Santos Queen Assumed to Heaven

O, dark flower
who says roses
don't come from ideas?

María Saturnina Sultry Yearning

The way skin holds us in
arching thoughts
and dreams like rainbows
between brain and bone
ovaries like twin moons
in darkness hang
while the heart tugs
a blazing sun
o compass rose
sister divine
water our gardens
let intuition flourish
let the feminine thrive

María Teresa Greatest Ancestor

They found you
in Park Chamizal
your body
beaten and strangled
your babe's milk
inside your breasts
still and white
in the midst of day
a holy night

María Victoria Reina de la Paz

Victoria was a queen
in England
no one killed her

someone
who uses a cell phone
and wears jeans
kills you

estas son la mañanitas
que cantaba el rey David
a las muchachas bonitas
se las cantamos así

despierta, mi bien despierta

yes, we sing it like this,
awaken, Beloveds, awaken!

see in the cracks
of your bodies
the light shining through

María

May the flower
of your birth
open up each day
receive into its depth
sun's honey rays
and at night
gently may it fold its petals
in sacred mystery
may it release its perfume
in sorrow as in joy
may its essence bloom for long
let us all remember
on this and every day
however compelling
words are not flesh
figurative language
life does not replace

Femicide Victims

For the purposes of this work only the names of victims whose first name was María were used. For a more complete listing of all the women killed visit: (http://www.thing.net/%7Ecocofusco/List.html)

María Agustina Hernández
María Ascención Aparicio Salazar
María Cristina Quezada Amador
María de Jesús Fong Valenzuela
María de Jesús González
María de la Luz Murgado G.
María de los Ángeles Acosta Ramírez
María de los Ángeles Alvarado Soto
María de los Ángeles Hernández Deras
María de Lourdes Galván Juárez
María del Refugio Núñez L.
María Maynez Sustaita
María del Rosario Cordero Esquivel
María Díaz Díaz
María E. Acosta Armendariz
María E. Luna Alfaro
María Elba Chávez
María Elena Chávez Caldera
María Elena Saucedo Meraz
María Estela Martínez
María Estela Martínez Valdez
María Eugenia Mendoza Arias
María Inéz Ozuna Aguirre
María Irma Blancarte Lugo
María Irma Plancarte
María Isabel Chávez G.
María Isabel Haro Prado
María Isabel Martínez González
María Isabel Nava Vázquez
María Isela Núñez Herrera
María López Torres
María Luisa Luna Vera
María Luisa y sus tres niños
María Maura Carmona Zamora
María Rocío Cordero Esquivel
María Rosa León Ramos

María Rosario Ríos y esposo
María Sagrario González Flores
María Santos Ramírez Vega
María Santos Rangel Flores
María Saturnina de León
María Teresa Rentería Salazar
María Victoria Arrellano Z.

Notes

The Litany of the Blessed Virgin Mary inspired the titles of the poems in this book. I combined the name of each victim I found whose name began with María with a line from this prayer. In some poems I use a poetic line instead of a line from the Litanies to accompany the woman's name. My hope is that this weaving of flesh and spirit creates a covenant of love and a place of survival and allegiance.

The Litany of the Blessed Virgin Mary

Lord, have mercy on us.
Christ, have mercy on us.
Lord, have mercy on us. Christ hear us.
Christ, graciously hear us.
God, the Father of heaven,
Have mercy on us.
God, the Son, Redeemer of the world:
Have mercy on us.
God, the Holy Ghost,
Have mercy on us.
Holy Trinity, One God,
Have mercy on us.
Holy Mary, pray for us.
Holy Mother of God,
Holy Virgin of virgins,
Mother of Christ,
Mother of divine grace,
Mother most pure,
Mother most chaste,
Mother inviolate,
Mother undefiled,
Mother most amiable,
Mother most admirable,
Mother of good counsel,
Mother of our Creator,
Mother of our Savior,
Virgin most prudent,
Virgin most venerable,
Virgin most renowned,
Virgin most powerful,
Virgin most merciful,
Virgin most faithful,

Mirror of justice,
Seat of wisdom,
Cause of our joy,
Spiritual vessel,
Vessel of honor,
Singular vessel of devotion,
Mystical rose,
Tower of David,
Tower of ivory,
House of gold,
Ark of the covenant,
Gate of Heaven,
Morning star,
Health of the sick,
Refuge of sinners,
Comforter of the afflicted,
Help of Christians,
Queen of angels,
Queen of patriarchs,
Queen of prophets,
Queen of apostles,
Queen of martyrs,
Queen of confessors,
Queen of virgins,
Queen of all saints,
Queen conceived without original sin,
Queen assumed into heaven,
Queen of the most holy Rosary,
Queen of peace.
[...]
V. Pray for us, O holy Mother of God.
R. *That we may be made worthy of the promises of Christ.*

Claudia Castro Luna served as Seattle's first Civic Poet from 2015-2017 and is the author of *This City* (Floating Bridge Press). She is a Hedgebrook and VONA alumna, the recipient of a King County 4Culture grant and a Jack Straw Fellow. Born in El Salvador, she came to the United States in 1981. She has an MFA in poetry, an MA in Urban Planning and a K-12 teaching certificate. Her poems have appeared in *Poetry Northwest, La Bloga, City Arts,* and *Taos Journal of International Poetry and Art,* among others. Her non-fiction work can be read in the anthologies, *The Wandering Song: Central American Writing in the US,* (Northwestern University Press); *Vanishing Points: Contemporary Salvadoran Narrative,* (Kalina Eds) and forthcoming in *This Is The Place: Women Writing About Home* (Seal Press). Living in English and Spanish, Claudia writes and teaches in Seattle where she gardens and keeps chickens with her husband and their three children.

Publications by Two Sylvias Press:

The Daily Poet: Day-By-Day Prompts For Your Writing Practice
by Kelli Russell Agodon and Martha Silano (Print and eBook)

The Daily Poet Companion Journal (Print)

Fire On Her Tongue: An Anthology of Contemporary Women's Poetry
edited by Kelli Russell Agodon and Annette Spaulding-Convy (Print and eBook)

The Poet Tarot and Guidebook: A Deck Of Creative Exploration (Print)

Killing Marías
by Claudia Castro Luna (Print and eBook)

The Ego And The Empiricist, Finalist 2016 Two Sylvias Press Chapbook Prize
by Derek Mong (Print and eBook)

The Authenticity Experiment
by Kate Carroll de Gutes (Print and eBook)

Mytheria, Finalist 2015 Two Sylvias Press Wilder Prize
by Molly Tenenbaum (Print and eBook)

Arab in Newsland , Winner of the 2016 Two Sylvias Press Chapbook Prize
by Lena Khalaf Tuffaha (Print and eBook)

The Blue Black Wet of Wood
by Carmen R. Gillespie (Print and eBook)

Fire Girl: Essays on India, America, and the In-Between
by Sayantani Dasgupta (Print and eBook)

Blood Song
by Michael Schmeltzer (Print and eBook)

Naming The No-Name Woman,
Winner of the 2015 Two Sylvias Press Chapbook Prize
by Jasmine An (Print and eBook)

Community Chest
by Natalie Serber (Print)

Phantom Son: A Mother's Story of Surrender
by Sharon Estill Taylor (Print and eBook)

What The Truth Tastes Like
by Martha Silano (Print and eBook)

Created with the belief that great writing
is good for the world.

Visit us online: www.twosylviaspress.com

Made in the USA
Lexington, KY
15 October 2017